The Leadership Deficit:

The Gap Between Strength and Vulnerability

JOSEPH URCAVICH

ISBN: 1507749481
ISBN 13: 9781507749487

ACKNOWLEDGMENTS

This book is a direct result of a thirty-year friendship that my wife, Arlis, and I have had with Ken and Chris Utech. Over the years we've cared for each other, cried together, fought on issues, shared vacations, dreamed, and worn each other out with various theories of living.

Every idea I've shared has been written about by individuals far more knowledgeable than me. They, however, did not have the privilege of running their internal disconnects and overall craziness through the grid of our unique and loving friends.

CONTENTS

Acknowledgments iii

Introduction vii

Chapter 1   Leading from Within 1

Chapter 2   Obstacles 11

Chapter 3   Success 21

Chapter 4   Risk 27

Chapter 5   Root Issues 32

Chapter 6   Shift 36

Chapter 7   When Will the Tension End? 42

Chapter 8   Why This Model? 48

Chapter 9   What Is Perseverance Based on? 53

Chapter 10   Staying the Course! 58

Final Thoughts 63

About the Author 67

INTRODUCTION

Every person I have had the privilege of sharing life with longs for relationships based on being known, being loved, and knowing that his or her emotions and thoughts matter.

Living in a state of relationship—in particular, intimate, heart-level communion with friends, workmates, or loved ones—requires a greater investment than most are willing to make. The hesitancy regarding making the investment is not based on the category of "want" as much as on the "method." Wanting something, or even being aware we need something, is not motivation enough to move toward what we feel needs to change. Procrastination and delay can become our methods of operation simply because we cannot envision a predictable outcome.

Years ago I went through a season of deep pain caused by broken trust between a workmate and myself. We attempted to close the distance but could not because both of us were attempting to assign blame on each other. The more intentional our efforts were to resolve the differences, the greater the distance became. Eventually it became unmanageable, and management asked him to find another job. Time and reflection have helped me recognize that we were both fighting for the wrong thing. We wanted justification for our actions. In doing so, we didn't fight for our relationship; instead, we both struggled to protect ourselves. That protracted battle cost us the primary ingredient we both longed for but were afraid to pursue: freedom—in particular, the freedom to accept another within an atmosphere of respect and understanding. The state we chose, out of ignorance, was emotional, self-imposed isolation—that's right, self-imposed.

How often has relational disappointment become the doorway to personal isolation?

I have come to believe that our relational model is the same in all areas of life. We can hide from the consequence of our model using position, power, or money to manipulate circumstances, but eventually the fruit of that model will confront us. Our doorway to isolation usually begins with an internal sense of being misunderstood or not known. Ultimately, the result of our model, unknown to others, leaves us with a sense of isolation. Developing leaders seek to know themselves, gaining internal clarity and direction first and then living that clarity before those within their influence.

In writing this book, I hope to give insight into several concepts that have guided my relational development. For over thirty years, I have worked directly with individuals, couples, and teams regarding their relational development. The basic concepts I have embraced and operated by have proven to give insight and options to people in various relational circumstances. The ideas I illustrate here are not unique; many others have written about these concepts. I will focus on illustrating what I have experienced and seen in my relationships with others. My hope is these practical ideas will challenge your insight and enhance your relationships.

1

LEADING FROM WITHIN

Success is not an accident.

— Tara VanDerveer

My parents expected me to behave in prescribed ways. I achieved results that pleased them, which gave us all a sense of accomplishment. My response to the cheers of an adoring crowd started early: take your first step, use the big potty, and button your own shirt. Every significant person around me applauded. This environment gave me a strong and consistent signal, which became a primary motivator for how I expected myself to live. I must become well educated, stay in shape, excel in my sport, marry a beautiful woman, drive a nice car, own an impressive house, raise smart kids, fill the bank account, and plan for retirement.

All good, but all externals meant to impress others and make me "acceptable." Years passed.

As moments of clarity began to attach themselves to each other, I saw that I had been groomed to climb but had not been warned that there was a major fissure in the landscape—one that I had no skills to avoid (much later I would call it a *values deficit*).

Instinctively, we seek approval at work by upping our levels of production. This gives only short-term satisfaction. By middle age we are stopped short by the curveballs life starts throwing. We strike out, hear the booing crowd, and trot back to the dugout, dejected and knowing we have failed in our performances. At that point, we feel a great need for understanding, love, and acceptance for who we are—not what we can or can't produce. Being groomed and reinforced by a performance-based society has done a number on us; our errors and outs in the game of life have simply revealed it.

Heartfelt expression requires us to move beyond cultural rules to honest, kind interaction. Until we learn to speak honestly with kindness, we tend to abdicate what we want or need emotionally for what will win approval. Few of us have been taught that leadership is not simply a role but a responsibility—one expressed through validating the value of those who follow us. Perhaps we are performing for the wrong audience. We believe those close to us will be accepting and supportive, which is often a false assumption. As we vie for the support of others, the rivalry often drives us to compete with those we love. Conflict ensues, and destruction begins—failure again.

Our option is to turn to the next level of support. We begin to play the game of life for those we can keep at arm's length: workmates, social contacts, and so on. But by doing so, we continue the process of performance and reinforce a faulty system that was actually put into place generations before us.

Question: How long can we sustain the game? When I was younger, my focus in life was oriented to taking care of others. Admirable, right? The problem with caregiving is that the caregiver gives off an aura that says, "I am OK; I have no needs." Caregivers actually believe that what they themselves long for cannot be expressed because it is selfish and immature. I never wanted people to know how selfish I felt even as I served others. I sensed they would reject me, so I pushed honesty into the shadows. I thought it was kept under wraps, but this fear tainted everything and every relationship. I had so many of my own needs going unacknowledged, unexplored, and, consequently, unmet. Because I had always been skilled at being a performance-based person, I was able to sustain the game for years. But when the pain of life outweighed the cheering crowds, I began to sense that the inner me was unknown—by me. The acceptance game had co-opted my life. I grew troubled enough to do some serious evaluation. Outside myself, I observed friends' marriages ending in divorce, leaving their families wounded and limping in a vacuum of intimacy. I determined to do all in my power to prevent that from happening to mine. It was to be a major shift.

All of us are co-opted by our culture. For instance, we have developed mobile technologies to feel connected even though we continue to feel further and further apart. I can risk myself anonymously on the web but am fearful of having the same dialogue with my partner, boss, or friend face-to-face. The technologically dominated society we embrace offers methods that feed into the fragmentation, and the resulting isolation leads to pseudo-relationships. The shallowness of performance-based living is felt through the fear many of us have regarding acceptance. The idea that if people knew what I really thought or saw my true ability or skill set, they would reject me—a haunting thought for many of us.

Question: What will it take to move out of this seemingly safe but unfulfilling pattern? The pain of not seeing value in myself beyond what was given through accomplishment forced me to look at who I was and what my life was really about. I had an urgency to discover what it took for relationships to flourish. In my search there emerged two necessary areas to explore: knowing myself and understanding my impact on others.

Question: Do you know who you are? I am not asking you to reflect on what you do but to investigate what motivates you. Society has taught us to identify ourselves by what we do (I am a teacher, doctor, etc.). It's not unusual to realize our career choice has been deeply influenced, directly or indirectly, by those we want to please—the cheering crowd. Two things to consider: Is it possible that we have chosen a future based on meeting someone's career expectations? Do we attempt to prove our worth by meeting the definition of *success* defined by our circle of influence?

Question: What happens internally to the individual who succeeds by pleasing his or her circle of influence? At some level, we have all tasted the bitter fruit of discontent. On its face, this doesn't make sense. It would seem that upon meeting the mark others have set, we would feel embraced and affirmed. In reality, we don't. That coveted sense of well-being remains out of reach, replaced by a crushing inner awareness: I am not valuable for who I am but only for how I measure up to others' stated goals. My excellent performance gives others a safe way to support me. Their support is a reward for my actions, but it leaves my identity untouched and undervalued. My self-worth internally erodes.

Question: What do we do when we sense the burn of personal discontent? To comfort ourselves, we look for weakness in someone else's performance and assign blame to it for our inadequacies. Our refusal to face and investigate our discontent keeps us stuck—unaware and immobilized for any meaningful relational growth. Not knowing who we are creates a relational mess.

Many years ago I met a man who had pursued a career to satisfy the expectations of his dad. He poured his life into what became a successful venture, and his father applauded his accomplishments. But the son struggled with discontent because he had put aside his own dreams in the hope of receiving love and acceptance from his dad. His success came at a huge cost: the fracturing of every relationship that was of value to him. These losses confirmed that he could not measure up.

The bitterness of not being able to do enough ripped at the core of his personal value and destroyed his confidence—his sense of self-value. Eventually, he gave up the career path he thought his dad wanted him to pursue and took on a position he thought was better suited to him.

The last chapter of his life has not been written, but the years after switching jobs did not give this man the satisfaction he craved. The pain of living too many years to please his dad and the losses that ensued left him so wounded that he was unable to discern who he was and whether he mattered. Because those two essential questions remained unanswered, he could only stumble ahead, searching for meaning in all the wrong places. His quest led him to a number of painful experiences, bad health, and more brokenness.

Question: How about the person who denies who he or she is? I met a man several years ago who was a hard-driving executive. He made business happen through amazing sales insight and strong goal setting. He chose to keep everything in his life neatly packaged, revealing to others just enough to be convincing. Throughout his life, people sensed they knew him, but there was no way to calculate how much because he revealed so little. He had put a lock on his relational encounters because he believed that the tender heart inside him was weakness. This hidden struggle robbed him of the opportunity to grow from the inside out and stole from those close to him the privilege of knowing how deeply tender he was. The potential of being seen as weak left him open to being misunderstood and isolated. His generosity and acts of compassion were missing full impact because he refused to allow others to know what he knew—he deeply cared and loved them and that drove his actions toward them. The acceptance and expression of his tenderness to those closest to him has begun a process of self-disclosure that will eventually permeate his entire life. Those close to him now know his loving heart and this expressed tenderness has made a difference.

Question: What can we do to effectively change our relational intentions and outcomes? The first step is to make a concerted effort to understand what drives us. I discovered that when my driving values were defined and authentically lived, I received honest responses from almost everyone with whom I engaged. Knowing your values allows you to restrain yourself from seeking to please as an emotional reaction. This is because understood values act as a governor on an engine. They restrain the impulse to give more than is healthy and productive. Values move us toward living consistently, regardless of circumstances, regardless of outcome.

Several years ago I had the privilege of speaking to the Corp of Engineers, Washington DC, on the subject of resilience. As part of that experience, I was able to spend an afternoon visiting the buildings that house our government. George Washington is captured in a wonderful painting in the rotunda of the US Capitol. He is seen handing over his commission papers to Congress and laying aside the power and position that his work as head of the Continental Army warranted. Some of his peers thought crowning him king would be a deserved culmination of his investment in America. But George lived by a creed—a value of selfless service. Leadership by power, force, and intimidation was what he had fought against. He had worked at establishing a republic using his authority and his ability to selflessly prioritize the welfare of those he loved and served. He gave up the sword and stepped down. His was the logical conclusion of a values-based life.

Question: Are we aware of how we impact people? Washington's values have had a profound influence on the United States for over two hundred years. His peers were willing and ready to accept his benevolent dictatorship; some even wished for an American monarchy. Washington valued the principles for which the Revolutionary War was fought, and he lived by that creed: personal responsibility, life, liberty, pursuit of happiness. How different America would have been if he had lived only for what he could gain in the moment. Values have ongoing generational effects. If our national values are clouded by actions simply meant to impress in the moment, self-centered agendas will dominate a divided population. Deciding to make a shift away from living for the moment and seeking purpose in our shared historical values appears to be countercultural. Leadership identifies values and should move those who follow toward the common good.

Question: Have you looked back generationally to understand how and why you live the way you do? When you see how your grandparents treated people, you have a better chance at understanding how and why your parents treated you and your siblings the way they did or still do. A generational perspective will give you important clues as to why you respond the way you do to others; it is deeply rooted in your family model. How men viewed women and women viewed men in the past—as well as the addictions, abuses, and successes and failures of those previous generations—have a startling impact on not just you but future generations.

As you gain a clearer view of what drives you, the patterns of your family will become a map that will show you why you've arrived at the place you're in. This generational map may also serve as an indicator that you are not headed in the right direction.

Realizing what you don't know will allow you the potential to disrupt generational patterns and refocus your positive driving values, moving you toward the life you long for.

Is it time for you to take a long, hard look at possible reasons you are living according to a faulty generational pattern?

Do you understand that the changes you make will give future generations a fighting chance to do life in a better way?

Do you want change bad enough to do the necessary work?

Observation: Until I am ready to seek out who I am and reveal my real self to others, I will never be truly known and loved.

2

OBSTACLES

Aim at heaven and you will get the earth thrown in. Aim at the earth and you will get neither.

— C. S. LEWIS

My observation is that most people grow up in a family that approaches life in one of two ways: (1) *organized*, which is calculated, where goals and expectations are the focus and are coupled with a high motivation to succeed; or (2) *disorganized*, which is based on survival, where little energy, money, or thought is put into decisions. Those who grow up in a highly structured environment can often present a success story that burns bright for a period of time until the relational disconnects begin to take their toll. Divorce, child custody issues, and financial tension are all the result of planning for and measuring success based on externals.

A friend of mine, Don, grew up in a highly organized family. His entire youth had been built on performance markers. From sports to business, he worked hard to prove himself and became extremely successful. But over time, even as he maintained success in the work world, the externals were powerless to heal the feeling of isolation within him.

Don was oblivious to the devastating impact he was having on his family. His wife was angry and bitter and felt undervalued to the point of despair. Eventually Don experienced what to him was the ultimate performance failure: a broken relationship. His wife left him for another man. The person she chose had none of Don's external success, but he listened to her, saw her value, and offered her respect. Had Don known then what he knows now, his marriage potentially could have been salvaged.

Don's new path began by seeking to uncover the disconnects that had begun very early in his highly organized childhood. He deliberately began to disentangle himself from the performance model by reconstructing his thought process. He now recognizes how vital it is to connect his personal values to all relationships and to be aware of how those values actually impact others.

It's true that the way we handle relationships transfers to all spectrums of our life, because we have basically one relational style with shades of nuance. I grew up in a disorganized environment. That model created its own unique issues. On the plus side, the uncertainty of an unstructured environment gave me a strong ability to accurately read the emotions of others. I learned early on how to read a room, and I'd work hard to create stability by using humor. People like me learn to intuitively direct their lives using gut instinct. The ideas of goal setting, linear planning, calculated risk, and programmed success are foreign. Those of us from disorganized families work hard at being recognized and give very little thought to the next step in a process we can't predict. Because we lack organization, our ship can wreck in a much more dramatic way when the energy required to perform for others runs out.

I worked with a woman whose life illustrated well the ramifications of a child growing up in a disorganized family. Hers was an alcoholic home, and she spent her childhood and teen years learning how to read her drunken mother. My workmate's well-being, and that of her siblings, was dependent on accurately anticipating what the mood was and how to best shape events. In the process, she suppressed her own emotions, feeling they mattered little in the survival process. Pressing on and making the best of the chaos became a deep pattern in her life.

Ironically, or should I say predictably, she married into the same type of environment. Her husband was addicted to alcohol and perpetuated the same kind of chaos as the single mother who had raised her. Eventually, this woman felt her gut could no longer be trusted. She had restricted her own emotion to the point of a total loss of self. Deeply exhausted and devoid of options, she reached out for help.

With amazement, she discovered that she had options that could move her beyond her experiences! She began by asking the following foundational question:

Question: Regardless of past experience, how do we move past what we already know? There is a first step in any process of change. Hers was the need to recognize what factors had robbed her of possessing sweet, childish vulnerability. Her natural development had been stunted to such a degree that she had little ability to attack the issues adults must face.

She and I discussed how the two of us, and a myriad of others who have personal deficits, have found the workplace to be an arena where we've been able to achieve a measurable degree of success. It's no wonder that folks like us gravitate to this external sense of gratification. But the pitfalls of this crutch are many. Depending primarily on work for fulfillment will inevitably lead to problems at home, such as being unengaged, preoccupied, self-centered, and surly. At work we can buckle down and make things happen; at home we are preoccupied and unavailable. At work we possess the ability to morph into an approachable and valuable teammate; at home we are who we are, and no member of the family is fooled—confused and frustrated, yes, but not fooled. Responsibilities are left for our partner to absorb. Hobbies, technology, and friends are easier than engagement with those we love. And the cycle continues. In its wake we are filled with regret, guilt, and shame.

It is predictable that we would protect ourselves both in the workplace and at home, haunted by the chance that someone will get a glimpse into our heart. We've been conditioned against being emotionally naked before anyone. Vulnerability frightens us away from a number of consistent behaviors. In our fear, we avoid; the possibility that we could be judged inadequate is too big a risk. We find ourselves alone, unknown, and uncertain, walking a path of pain toward maturity. Unless we learn how to invest honest love and commitment, we will be robbed of the chance to give our hearts to those we love. We'll miss out. They'll miss out.

Some people produce a similar result by following another path. These folks tend to hide their emotional isolation by filling their schedule with social activity. For this crowd, shopping, clubs, the gym, volunteer opportunities, remodeling of the house, church activities, and the busyness of children satisfy, to some small degree, the ever-present hunger to measure up—to be loved for who they are. Even professionals in the psychological field who experience success in the workplace admit that emotional isolation is the sore spot in their life. Ultimately, all of us want to have a voice and a life that matters to those around us. We all want to be known for who we are and be loved anyway.

Question: How do we leave behind the patterns we have? We have to face our biggest fear: honesty. As a young man, when I chose to operate dishonestly with myself and others, relational isolation existed. Until I could admit that my life was bound by fear of being known and judged, I couldn't understand the role dishonesty played in keeping me at arm's length from others. It's important for you to know that my parents were good people; they never abused me. Nor was I the victim of consistent bullying. I suffered no more than any other kid in my school and neighborhood. And yet I had a very real fear of others knowing that inside of me lived an imposter. I saw no option other than protecting myself with an armor of sports, friends, and humor. Changing this pattern took years of rubbing shoulders with mature men and women who were brutally honest about where they saw my life headed. Their investment allowed me to close the hole in my heart regarding trust. They believed in me.

A new day dawns when we tap into the experiences that have caused this fear. Too often we focus on the event or circumstance that produced the emotion, but the impact it has had is more critical to understand. The following example might clarify this.

I had a friend whose dad used him as a means to gain his own significance. This young man had to act a certain way, have the right attitudes, and make the right decisions. The way his dad micromanaged his life left his son immobilized and unable to make even small decisions. Until this young man had the courage to speak with his dad about his feelings of incompetence, he was trapped by the words and thoughts his dad stated to his childhood mind.

Trauma of all kinds, verbal or physical, can create a pattern of isolation, a sense of worthlessness, a lack of self-love. It's what we do with events like these that ultimately build a lifestyle. The importance of putting our pain-filled events and the fear they produce into context opens a wonderful internal door. It is at that moment we begin to find forgiveness, self-love, and freedom.

Question: What does it mean to forgive? Forgiveness has to do with releasing the one who has caused you pain from having emotional control over your life. You acknowledge the impact of that person's actions and, within the context of your own weakness, recognize that you also have the capacity to wound others, maybe even in the same way. The event you experienced will never go away and should never be denied. It will stand as a guard over your heart in new relationships as well as a safe zone between you and the person who hurt you.

If the perpetrator of the offense wishes another chance at relationship, the person must own and verbalize how he or she has wounded you. The individual will need to face the reality of his or her behavior without minimizing his or her actions. Ownership over past actions and a sincere apology can go a long way toward reopening fractured or closed relationships. Having said that, some injuries are too grievous for the restoration of relationship to take place. Ownership of the offense may be offered and received, but the wound will not allow for trust to be reestablished.

While we all long for others to extend grace for our failures, we tend to protect our hearts and be slow to show that same grace to others. Facing who we are, what we have done, what we are capable of, and how we wish to live has a way of humbling us enough to drop the arrogance of needing to be right. I am a person who has a difficult time eating, sleeping, or relaxing if I know my actions have wounded someone. The old adage "Confession is good for the soul" is true for me. On many occasions I have been forced by conscience to apologize for my deeds. I am convinced that most people we have offended or hurt want resolution and peace as much as we do. In my experience, the power of forgiveness has provided hope for a restorative process.

Question: What does it mean for you to love you? Most people shy away from this important issue because it's narcissistic on its face. We have all been around emotionally immature people who are preoccupied with self-importance, and we don't care for their company. But let's look at it another way.

Real self-love, a deep understanding of one's worth, is foundational to loving others. If we find worth in ourselves, true value and respect can be communicated to others. If we do not love ourselves, the internal spirit of self-rejection will resound in all our relationships. We may like ourselves, since liking is closely tied to performance and how others evaluate us, but the capacity to love and accept ourselves is based on who we are and the character that is resident in us.

Today's societal standards of how we look, what we own, where we live, the trips we take, and the cars we buy all support a faulty performance-based type of love. It is superficial and leaves us floundering for a sense of personal freedom.

Question: What is freedom? Freedom is the ability to express who we are, what we think, and particularly what we feel without a fear of rejection. It is an emotional place in life where we know what we value and how to express what we value in a tone that can be heard. It is not about getting what we want, but rather about having a willingness to give of ourselves in appropriate ways. Personal freedom is found when we no longer fear how we will be perceived. We embrace the person we are and clearly present that person to the individuals around us. Learning how to release ourselves to others can be a confusing process because we take the risk of wrong perception and mischaracterization...or we do it badly. As you journey the road to freedom, remember to control the only things you can: your words, your tone, and your heart.

Question: Are you feeling a disconnect between your head and your heart? It's amazing how many people know intellectually what to do but lack the internal confidence to risk themselves for the life they desire. Vulnerability and risk are necessary to internal growth.

Observation: The direction of life is not based on the kind of environment in which one grew up; it is the honesty with which one appraises that environment that matters.

3

SUCCESS

We must become the change we want to see.

— MAHATMA GANDHI

I had the privilege of hanging around the fringe of professional football for nine years. I witnessed a number of decisions that fans and friends of the organization did not like. Ultimately, football decisions boil down to replacing competence with an unknown. Knowing without proven data, acting confidently without assurance, and committing in the face of potentiality are marks of successful leaders in all walks of life.

Question: What has allowed some leaders to be consistently effective? There are several key ingredients, but knowing how to work hard and honestly follow one's gut is the place to start. I have observed that there is a common attitude that wise leaders share: Don't follow me because I am appointed a leader. Follow me because I demonstrate leadership through my effort and willingness to risk myself. Leaders are those individuals who, through choice, position, or circumstances, are required to make decisions that shape the environment of those around them. True leaders risk themselves to enrich others in the home, in the work environment, and across society.

Positional leadership and organic leadership are additional ways to explain the methods used by those who lead. Positional leadership is utilized in the military, many large corporations, family businesses, and even volunteer-based organizations. It can be based on seniority, blood, or association. Its weakness is that it allows for the inexperienced and uncommitted to climb the ranks, and positional power is often maintained through threat and fear of reprisal.

Organic leadership, in my experience, follows another path. It begins with an individual being committed to developing, inspiring, and managing him- or herself. Organic leaders gain their authority by sacrificing themselves for the well-being of those who would follow them. They choose the path of risk and vulnerability. In short, they are relational. People believe in this kind of leader, and they gladly follow.

Question: What factor can short-circuit the process? We ourselves can sabotage what we desperately want to accomplish. It may look like this: We hesitate, waiting for the right personnel, work environment, marriage partner, and money or time allotment. We delay taking responsibility, using any excuse we believe will legitimize our inaction. Bottom line: We see ourselves as victims of external forces. We live out a self-imposed position of disempowerment and never realize our potential.

To prevent this personal disaster, we must step past fear of both success and failure. It begins internally. My personal struggle revolved around accepting myself as competent and sensing some people wanted to be close to me because they liked me. My mind got the accomplishment idea, but being embraced for who I was caused real internal unrest. It was particularly tough for me to envision how to change internally. I had lived my younger years using external clues as a means to function, and this had become a deeply entrenched habit. Sustaining a practical awareness of self took time and some wise counsel from friends to effectively implement.

Question: What are the foundational attitudes for effective relational leadership? Two attitudes are basic and essential: the need to be inclusive of people and their ideas and the desire to set a tone of purpose. Both are necessary. Inclusion is a prerequisite in achieving our purpose. The level of investment (time, money, etc.) may vary, but there should be no doubt in any teammate's mind that he or she is vital to his or her leader. A solid leader intuitively knows how to create a sense of value in those he or she serves. Genuine affirmation, continual recognition of contributions, a respect for any and all suggestions, and a working knowledge of teammates' families and life situations are all essential to inclusion.

In any organization, family, or social group, there are those who fly under the radar. Much of the time, it is because they minimize themselves; they contribute but do not see worth in either themselves or their effort. A wise leader seeks them out and includes them under his or her umbrella of influence. The tone is unmistakable: everyone matters to the success of the organization.

When the leader at work interacts with me, I feel good—important. I perform my responsibilities at an enhanced level. My job may be in maintenance, but my value as a team member, validated publically by the leader, will result in a cleaner work environment. Worth and performance go hand in hand, resulting in a more socially secure workplace—an environment in which each employee can function and grow. Camaraderie in the business environment will be the natural by-product.

As an inexperienced leader, my micromanaging style disempowered my subordinates. Of course, I took that style home. I caused my wife to feel unappreciated, and I confused my children by implying unrealistic expectations. I had to face the fact that I was leading poorly in every arena of my life. When I finally saw it for what is was, I was humbled and ready to lead differently.

I began to include coworkers in a process that validated their contribution. The office became a place of freedom—freedom to dream, create, and grow. I didn't just feel the change; I saw the effects and heard feedback that offered proof of the new atmosphere. The same was true at home. I brought my wife into all major decisions and empowered her to control any area she felt confident in. I began to consistently voice my love and appreciation for her efforts. It did not diminish me; it actually made me more valuable and lovable to her. My children also benefitted from a dad who could admit his failure, apologize, and allow them to speak directly about any issue where I had confused or disappointed them.

Question: How does one set a tone? The first question is, what kind of tone are you setting now? It took me years before I recognized that I set a definite tone with those I met, lived with, worked with, and so on. I may not have known the kind of tone I set, but all those who felt it certainly knew. An issue that surfaced in my work environment was that most subordinates would rarely risk telling me the kind of tone I set. Why? Did I intimidate them with my personality and confidence? I began to see that I needed their honesty— I needed their help to know the truth about the tone I set.

Years later, I am even more convinced that what leaders think of themselves is often quite different from the perception others have of them. They may feel they lead by inclusion and acceptance, when the truth is they exclude and alienate.

I believe that in order to consistently set a tone of inclusion, a leader must recognize the need to love those being led. I am not speaking of a romantic view of love but of a heartfelt choice to prioritize the needs of others before yours. It is difficult to prioritize others' deep needs without including them in an honest dialogue. In a family, your spouse and children need to know you have placed their well-being above your own. They want to believe you will choose to sacrifice yourself for them. When we prioritize others by loving them in practical ways and making their needs a priority, they feel the difference. If their success is as vital to us as our own success, it creates a dynamic of shared responsibility, which results in shared success. The real value of a love-based tone is that all those who experience it realize they matter and are valued, and the result is a confidence in undertaking the task together.

Observation: Inclusion through tone setting is what rallies your team to own one another's success.

4

RISK

*Coming together is a beginning. Keeping together
is progress. Working together is success.*

— HENRY FORD

In almost every endeavor, there are obstacles to sustaining success. This is a truism when speaking of relationships. In almost any family, business, or social group, the issue that causes the most distress is not the plan or system; it is the breakdown in relationship.

A family can be functioning reasonably well when tensions over who-knows-what begin to develop. At that point, one of the family leaders defines the issue. Disagreement ensues on what the real problem is, and all hell breaks loose. Time passes, tensions mount, the kids act out, and there can even be talk of separation or divorce.

In the workplace, production can be up and the plant running smoothly, but for whatever reason, tensions begin to build. Management believes it is the fault of inflexible workers; workers think management is pushing too hard and not paying them enough. In an incredibly brief time, individuals are labeled, sides are taken, a strike is called, and work becomes a place of chaos. We have all seen or been a part of this scenario.

Question: What triggers the fundamental disconnect? As a young man, I strove for success but didn't know how to handle being successful. Actually, I was profoundly afraid of it. Since it had been drummed into me that failure should never be allowed to dominate or disrupt my life, I was afraid of that, too. So for me, fear of failure proved easier to handle than fear of success. Just the sound of the word *success* filled me with anxiety. It was something I longed for, but at the same time, I could not predict the cost and definition of success.

Here is how it works in my world: I make a decision to change how I have approached others. I have thought it through and have a strong intellectual grasp on what is required to make and sustain fundamental change. I cruise along enjoying the fruit of my intellectually induced process, but then something happens, often unanticipated. An event takes place that roadblocks the change I desire. In my case it usually involves a personal goal that is laid aside for some self-protective purpose. The regret and sense of failure are immediate. This is a deeply internal process with emotional consequences. I immediately associate the current challenge with past failures. Of particular concern is any unanticipated relationship tension. Instead of moving along the path I have chosen toward the unknown uncontrollable, I fall back on past experiences, opt for what I know, and leave behind the fear of the unknown and uncontrollable. Being able to predict or control seems more important in that moment than the goal I had driven toward.

I knew an athlete who feared success. He had all the physical abilities to perform at the highest level of his sport but was unable to persevere through the slightest difficulty. Ironically, he looked for situations that would allow him to take time away from workouts, practice, and ultimately fame and financial reward. What could have been was lost to the fear of success. He became a victim of injury. It excused him from risking all he had to gain what he could not control. Being close to the goal and sustaining control seemed more compelling than risking it all for a greater reward.

Question: Why would we opt for predictability? Self-protection. Risk taking is dangerous territory, and I know that from experience. When I've approached another with vulnerability—risking myself to accomplish a deep connection—rejection, ridicule, and isolation were often the result. I learned early in life that my heart is vulnerable—the very reason I savored short-term accolades of performance and getting attention for what I did rather than for who I was. An attitude of "let others love me for what I can do, not for who I am" gave me a false sense of security, but it seemed to carry less risk. I was haunted by the thought, "If they know who I am, they will not like me, much less love me." This attitude was confirmation of my own self-rejection.

On my continued journey toward openness, I can now state, "It is tough to risk truly loving another if we don't love ourselves." Heart protection is the preoccupation of most of us, because we don't know how to discover love for self. Safety is fickle; it captures us as prisoners of our own fear. Self-love is not a narcissistic preoccupation with self. It is an acceptance, warts and all, that allows us to embrace our humanity and celebrate the impact we have on those around us. If we choose to own the successes, we need to be willing to own the failures.

There is a strong indicator that lets me know that I effectively love myself: I no longer base the evaluation of my contribution on self-counsel. I now engage others through my presence. This means being with others, allowing them to know my thoughts, risking myself to confront tension, and being vulnerable when I have wounded another. There is nothing predictable about this.

Question: Is there a way out of this fear-based cycle? There is a way out, and it involves more than managing our emotions and thought processes. It involves an understanding of the generational patterns, passed down from grandparents to parents to children, which have haunted us all. Unless we develop a keen desire to disrupt and close down these patterns, they will subconsciously direct and shape our lives.

Observation: Clarity regarding the personal motivators in our lives allows us the potential to understand and defeat our fear-based patterns.

5

ROOT ISSUES

*Once you'd resolved to go, there was
nothing to it at all.*

— JEANNETTE WALLS

To find and live in freedom requires a willingness to recognize what inhibits our heart and restricts the airways of our emotional breath. For many of us, the freedom we long for seems out of reach, unable to be fully realized. It isn't. Freedom is an attitude of living in reality, unwilling to be controlled or defined by the unknown.

Question: Is there a pathway toward greater freedom? Yes. Moving in the direction of internal freedom requires a willingness to confront our fears. The journey begins by engaging in relationships that matter. Engaging means putting our entire person—good, bad, and ugly—into the mix of community with the person or persons we are pursuing. It does not mean that the details of our failure and our lack of discipline need to be fully known, but an understanding or awareness of that failure needs to be shared.

Years ago I risked myself; I sought a deeper friendship with a highly skilled professional. It became apparent after several hours of conversation that he was unwilling to share at a personal level. His method of dialogue was to keep all the relational energy focused on a topic he controlled. This created a tension I couldn't handle. Sadly, I had to walk away from a potential friendship because it would have trivialized my longing for depth. Risking oneself does not always result in getting what we long for. But without the risk, the potential of more would never be known.

Question: How can tension be handled? Personal issues that are potential points of conflict need to be on the table—right out in the open for all to see. In the workplace, if someone decides to own the tension alone, it will lead to team disruption. Sharing the tension allows teammates to equally acknowledge what the issue is and what needs to be owned. Remember that most teams and individuals work very hard to avoid and excuse relational tensions. When a relational environment is transparent, safety is the result. This gives everyone on the team the freedom to discuss, identify, and move toward the accomplishment of the goal. Teamwork dissipates both hidden and overt tension.

Communication that is kind and promotes community is another critical factor in the quest for freedom. Words matter, but tone matters more. When we say what needs to be said honestly, with authenticity and with kindness, it allows relationships to flourish and become the foundation of successful, shared accomplishment. A number of years ago, I sat down with a subordinate I knew was struggling. I asked him how satisfied he was in his current position, and if he could do whatever he desired in the organization, what would that be? He quickly shared how frustrated and displaced he felt in his job. His desire was to be a primary leader, but within our organization, that was not an option. The tone I used to draw out of him what he really wanted was one of respect. I wanted him to succeed with me or somewhere else, so I carefully provided a way for him to leave gracefully to pursue a bigger vision. Over the next three months, together we found an opportunity outside our organization that could fulfill his desire to lead. We remain friends and confidants to this day.

Freedom, tension sharing, and kind communication lead to an atmosphere of redemptive relationship. Those who have been ostracized by unexpressed emotions or an inability to see their weaknesses can often, but not always, be brought back to a place of productive inclusion. We do our best to heal and restore the dignity of others, but then we must leave the ball in their court.

Observation: We all long for someone to invest in us by accepting who we are and validating that we matter.

6

SHIFT

There is a certain relief in change, even though it be from bad to worse. As I have found in traveling in a stagecoach, that it is often a comfort to shift one's position, and be bruised in a new place.

— WASHINGTON IRVING

Question: Is a paradigm shift necessary? Absolutely. however, individuals and organizations rarely make a change until discomfort becomes so great that the status quo is unsustainable. Pain in all areas of life has a unique ability to grab and hold our attention. As long as it exists, we are riveted by its intensity and are on a constant search to resolve it. In my experience, most of us try to find solutions that allow us to maintain control without expending the effort necessary to be free of the chokehold.

Years ago I ruptured a disc in my back. The pain was intense, and I sought relief in many ways. As a final act of desperation, I went to my doctor and begged for back surgery. He stopped me short and said, "The kind of cutting needed to fix this problem may or may not lead to the conclusion you desire." He suggested I wait a year to find out what my body would do. During that year my body began to heal the painful disc. Within two years I was back to all my normal activities. Pain management and resolution can mean knowing the options but waiting to see how things naturally work themselves out. Activity does not always lead to accomplishment.

Question: What does the process of a relational paradigm shift look like? After self-appraisal, self-love/acceptance, and kind communication comes the most difficult but significant step: laying a foundation for the shift through the relational tone we set. The primary concept that must drive and center our tone-setting effort is a realization that relationship is the mechanism by which life principles get explored and refined. The average person desires a relational formula that states, "Do this or that, and here is the prescribed outcome." It's not that simple.

The ingredients of relational understanding are universal, but their implementation is an art form. The shape of our relational reality is defined by who we include in the discussion. Those whom we allow to speak directly into our life and those who modeled our relationships in the past set the stage for our current relational choices. Ironically, so much of what we do relationally is done in our heads, which is a solo undertaking that excludes others. We function that way to protect ourselves, but in reality we isolate, and the result is tension. Without others involved in the dialogue, the opposite of what we intend occurs. We become or remain defensive, immature, self-centered, insecure personalities.

The concept of setting a relational tone can be difficult to grasp because it seems cold and hurtful to tell someone the truth. When it comes to evaluating another's performance, abilities, talents, skill sets, character traits, or values, we will often be less than honest rather than risk offending the person. Because we operate this way, both of us get hurt. We cheat our friends by withholding. We hurt our friends by not giving them information that could be helpful or even essential.

Question: What are the basic elements of truth telling? A truism: I know what I know, but there is much more to know than what is known. As my friend Ken Utech taught me, a healthy attitude toward this step is to embrace this simple principle: share your heart with others. Being right is not the issue; being honestly engaged is. His advice was right on target.

We evaluate each other in every conversation. We agree and disagree as we talk. Questioning, evaluating, and, on occasion, discarding unusable information are necessary for a growing relationship. Ideas can motivate if we embrace them as instruments of change that should be weighed and sorted. Our perception is that we hear them as demands because of the isolation model that most of us have chosen in order to self-protect. There is no need to be defensive or angry over a need for clarity.

I have a small group of close friends who have proven to be trustworthy when dealing with me. I have invited them to tell me exactly what they feel and think about me. They may critique my behavior or choices, but they will still affirm their love and concern for me. They have given my life insight, even in the most difficult circumstances. They are rarely 100 percent right, but I will take 60 percent from a friend who loves me and discard the rest.

Question: How does one implement effective tone setting? Remember, tone setting has to do with us. In laying a foundation for relational change, we must be the change before we can bring the change. The process of tone setting must seep gradually into all of our relationships. Too often there is a tendency to declare what is going to happen rather than living out what we desire to see happen. Patience and perseverance are necessary in this first stage of development.

Question: What is the biggest roadblock at this stage of change? We are! The desire for change can overwhelm a rational view of how gradually it comes about. We want it so badly that we can attempt to force the process. Usually this meets with some strong opposition. Far too often the initiator gets frustrated, throws in the towel, and sees his or her good intentions thwarted by ungrateful teammates. If we want to see change, we need to model the change we desire. All of the ingredients we have talked about—being vulnerable, loving yourself, taking risks, and so on—need to be practiced before they will be understood and incorporated by others. Again, patience and perseverance are needed to stay the course.

Question: How can intentional tone setting be sustained? Slow down and first change yourself. When you come up against a challenge, embrace the truth in what is said without being defensive. When people experience tension, they often speak in self-protective terms that push all the responsibility toward the force that is seeking change. Do not become a victim by beginning to list in your mind reasons why this process won't work. Stay focused on your goal, and work patiently to accomplish tone setting. Live who you choose to be!

Question: When is it time to include others? If we follow through in establishing a tone of acceptance and inclusion, others will feel drawn toward the direction our life is headed. Everyone wants to be valued and included, and to sense ownership. When a person of influence sets the tone for those attitudes, others are brought into the process.

When others acknowledge the new environment, we will recognize a paradigm shift has taken place.

Observation: Through loving oneself, a person can set a tone of inclusion that will affect his or her circle of influence.

7

WHEN WILL THE TENSION END?

*Body tension will always be present if our good
feeling is just ordinary, self-centered happiness.
Joy has no tension in it, because joy accepts
whatever is as it is.*

— CHARLOTTE JOKO BECK

"Happily ever after" is the last line of fairy tales. It doesn't
happen at work, with close friends, or in a marriage. There
may be seasons of harmony, but where there is passion,
there is tension. Regardless of the venue, investment in
a relationship guarantees that tension will exist. What we
do with it is most important. Let me say it another way:
if there is a complete absence of tension with others,
their significance to you is minimal. In my dialogue with

married couples over the years, it has always surprised me that they view tension and the anger that ensues as a billboard declaring relational failure. Nothing could be further from the truth.

Question: Where does relational tension come from?

At times our tension comes from feeling something that's been unexpressed by another—the elephant in the room. This tension feels covert and destructive. At work as well as in families, we can go years—even a lifetime—feeling tension but never knowing its source because no one has the courage to address it. It will not simply go away. If we're lucky, another tension will enter the picture, and all hell will break loose. Finally offenses will be declared, which is hard but good, because then we have something to work with. With everything on the table, we can ask the tough questions and give each person present a chance to air his or her grievances. Respect each perspective, give yours, and be humble enough to apologize.

Much of the time, we fall back on interpreting the tension through our self-defensiveness. This viewpoint may or may not be accurate, but until we have a means to lay out our emotional perspective, the tension will exist without discovery or understanding. We have all felt the awkwardness of walking into an existing conversation and knowing that our entrance was not desired. The reason may have nothing to do with us, but we will interpret it as rejection. We assume, "They must have been talking about me," or "I must not be good enough to be included in their conversation." Most often we are wrong on both accounts, but when we don't have an accurate, objective explanation, we think through the lens of our insecurity. This response is most likely based on a poor self-image, but it can be focused and brought to light through relationships built on trust. Our tendency is to dismiss judgmental words when said by a person who has no clout in our lives, but when communicated by a trusted loved one, such words produce intense emotion. Context does matter when language is involved.

Question: How can tension with others be handled? This question assumes we are responsible to make the tension disappear. In order to handle the tension effectively, we must make relational balance the ultimate goal. In most relationships one partner is overly responsible for the health and well-being of the relationship, while the other partner tends to take less responsibility for the same. One of them works hard to maintain life and joy; the other simply receives and only gives back when forced by circumstances to do so. This way of managing relationships is unbalanced and has a relatively short shelf life.

On most occasions, when a couple comes for marital advice, the appointment is set up by the woman. The man agrees to come with the hope and expectation that his wife will be enlightened. The far-too-common scenario looks like this: The unhappy wife is overly responsible, mothering and managing their children as well as an inadequately prepared and irresponsible man who is used to being taken care of. She's had it! When words haven't worked to express her exhaustion and utter frustration, she's resorted to weapons: belligerence, berating, silence, sexual withdrawal, and, in extreme cases, violence. He doesn't get it: he works hard and has unmet expectations that cause an attitude of disapproval and rejection to dominate his attitude.

Question: How should an overly responsible person handle his or her emotional exhaustion? Recognize this is often the norm. Most relationships have this kind of imbalance. Understand that as long as you are willing to carry the tension, the other person will gladly let you do it. That person may or may not be aware of the emotional burden he or she has placed on you. First, realize that you can only change yourself. Second, figure out what you have done or currently do that allows the other to escape sharing the emotional load. Sharing the load means exploring or questioning reasons why the partner is unable or unwilling to follow through on expectations they have agreed to.

Question: How is ownership of over responsibility best expressed? This is where tension management becomes an art form. When a dilemma, which is some form of tension, invades the relationship, don't emotionally react. Seek to determine the origin of the tension—is it your doing or that of another person? If your MO is being overly responsible, your gut and the irresponsible person will push the quivering emotional mess toward you. Don't readily accept it. Analyze it closely, and recognize what's happening. If you are the cause, own it and apologize. If it truly is coming from the other individual, moving the tension back toward balance is an appropriate response. The shift could be as simple as asking if the other person feels tension and what he or she believes it is about.

Children push tension toward parents all the time. "It's not fair. I am tired. You don't love me"—childish, emotional tension makers. Ironically, we adults resort to the same exact words! The way to bring balance is by pursuing the "why" for the feelings being expressed. Asking questions and listening to answers is showing great respect. In discovering the reasons, we include the feelings and input of the child or partner who is distressed. Somehow, when inclusion takes place, shared responsibility is often the result.

Question: How does one make better use of questions? Questions tend to be an ideal way to awaken an irresponsible person. Sincere inquiry sets a tone of respect and value for the one who must answer. His or her opinion is being sought out, his or her investment is critical, and he or she matters to the person asking the questions. If the interaction is listening based, without judgment of emotions or reasons to think differently, real value can be gained. Once the person's value is assured, he or she will more willingly help identify the source of the tension. At that point, the person's added input will lead toward a discussion of a resolution that will satisfy both parties. When a solution is reached, a new relational pattern starts to emerge. Awareness followed by relational finesse has the best chance of producing an environment where tension is more quickly resolved.

Observation: Control or freedom, power or authority— the latter in each case is based on loving oneself so we are freed to love others.

8

WHY THIS MODEL?

Everyone thinks of changing the world, but no one thinks of changing himself.

— LEO TOLSTOY

We live in a culture of blame and in a state of disappointment. Lawsuits, the ultimate cultural lottery, have become a common theme in most of our lives. We complain about the legal option until we can push the blame for something onto the plate of another. Once our expectations have gone unrealized or accidents have disrupted our lives, we resort to blaming someone—anyone besides ourselves. We search for a way to make someone else pay.

Disappointment often becomes the state we live in, pervading our private and professional lives. It doesn't take many years to begin noticing a disturbing pattern; we're not performing up to our expectations in either tasks or relationships. There's got to be something or someone to blame. We can point at inadequate income, our inept co-workers, or faulty management. On the home front, our frustrations must be the fault of our spouse, kids, extended family, or even neighbors. The joyous freedoms we desired and expected to find in the home, with friendships, and at work are colored by a gray cloud of discontent that is brought on by long-term disappointment.

Question: How can a person stand against the on-slaught of blame and the state of discontentment in order to find personal freedom? Standing up for oneself is always countercultural. Seeing and accepting yourself for who you are and sharing honestly with those around you brings a sense of personal freedom. By *freedom* I mean the desire we all have to be known for who we are and loved. Self-love is highly underrated. We see it as a nega-tive, but when you love yourself—the good, the bad, and the ugly—you are free to love those around you. Healthy self-love includes coming to terms with your strengths and weaknesses, good and bad behaviors, and successes and failures. It enables you to stand against the culture and deal with inner discontent.

Question: What will implementation of these ideas produce? Keep your eye on the goal. Always remember: the process is about not what you do but who you are becoming. You are moving toward being a responsible, risk-taking, vulnerable engager of relationship. The tone you set will be radically different from those around you. Some people will seek to undercut the tone you are moving toward. They will find it threatening and very uncomfortable. Stay focused. Be kind. Give everyone in your circle of influence the opportunity to witness a relational leader who understands the dynamic of authority.

Question: Wait a minute—we just went from tone setting to authority. Are you advocating manipulation of others? Actually, the opposite is true. Healthy authority is about freedom being exercised to benefit all in your sphere of influence. It is power under control. Authority by this definition is about freely sacrificing yourself so others can benefit from the atmosphere you create.

Question: Whose stock goes up when people realize they have met a leader who values them above him- or herself? Bingo, right on—it is the leader's! It is a validation of that leadership.

Historically, we know this works. Gandhi and Martin Luther King Jr. are two of many leaders who put personal sacrifice and authority ahead of power and position. They won because their ideas moved their generations and those to come. The basic message of both men was this: know and respect yourself. Their leadership was validated as those who followed moved past the uncertainty of outcome. They trusted their leader. Neither Gandhi nor King could have led with authority unless they first saw value in loving and believing in themselves. With that confidence, they were willing to risk the self-sacrifice because they could envision the outcome.

Question: Why would people want to follow a self-sacrificing leader? Following an unselfish leader gives people a safe place for creating and producing. A leader who exhibits this type of authority must provide a safe round table. It will become the forum for expressions of opposing opinions, fears, and personal preferences. No ridicule or outright rejection is acceptable. That being said, only an emotionally strong leader can take the critique of others and stay engaged, creating a safe place for even misplaced emotion to be expressed.

Question: What is misplaced emotion? It is emotion that comes from a deep well dug by past offences and disappointments. Even when we don't recognize it as coming from that source, we draw strength from that emotion to fortify us against more hurt, and we use it to force change.

When misplaced emotion erupts in a family or office setting, a wise leader recognizes it for what it is, because he or she has already waded through personal waters of pain from past hurts and arrived at the shore of emotional safety and stability. The leader is now able to see each person who is in his or her sphere as a cistern of past hurts and distrusts. He or she can then share personal struggles in an attempt to help another or a group move past using misplaced emotion to disrupt and force change.

Observation: A personal tone of accepting change, embracing sacrifice, and providing safety is the ultimate condition we are working toward.

9

WHAT IS PERSEVERANCE
BASED ON?

*Even if I knew that tomorrow the world would go
to pieces, I would still plant my apple tree.*

— Martin Luther King Jr.

A critical question we face when contemplating change
has to do with its timeline. "How long will this take?"
is closely followed by, "Will I get what I want out of
this deal?" The deeper question should be, "What will
it take to stop me in my quest to better myself?" At some
point the answer you provide will reveal your true motivation. Without question, perseverance—the ability to
stay the course—is based on an internal reservoir of resilience. This is an internal ability to see the world from

an optimistic perspective, to recognize that setbacks are temporary, and to be able to have an attitude of gratefulness in good and tough times. Resilience is fundamentally the ability to respond to change under duress.

Question: What qualities are vital to living a resilient life? The character qualities of integrity, authenticity, and humility are keys to becoming resilient. First and foremost, integrity is essential—the ability to look inside and see one's strengths and weaknesses with some objectivity. To lay yourself bare, internally, provides a context for self-acceptance as well as a platform from which to have honest interactions with those around you. Integrity is essential to building a trustworthy life.

Second, one needs to be authentic. Authenticity develops when you risk yourself, allowing others to know you beyond performance. In your desire to interact honestly through both your strengths and weaknesses, you allow trusted people to come alongside and share what they see. Resilience can further develop when you embrace sound advice and then make the necessary changes to live an authentic life.

Finally, one must be humble. Humility is recognizing that your strengths must be under control. When that is in place, you allow others the opportunity to shape and contribute to a process (expect that you may have to fight against your skill set and past patterns that would prefer to forge ahead alone). Welcoming others to contribute is vital. This inclusion requires humility and is a relational multiplier that reinforces resilience.

Question: How does one balance the tension between motive and outcome? I have found the context for all self-investigation is rooted in the premise that we tend to perform rather than reflect. From the time we are infants, everything we do is applauded. From the first step to using the big potty, the reward for success becomes apparent. It's not who we are that matters but what we do.

Pleasing others brings reward when you are younger, but it leads to frustration as you mature and desire to be valued for who you are. Challenging performance as a motive requires a purposeful introspection through a sustained inside look. In my case, doing so allowed me to see more clearly the consequences of my motives and helped me evaluate what certain outcomes had cost me. Personal relief—an eased internal tension—was gained when I was able to see my past in this context. It continues to give me better insight when I make daily choices.

Question: How does one give honestly to others without creating more tension? You will need to determine what it means to take courageous action. To have insight and opinions and not share them is to cheat those closest to you. We've learned that relationships that are valued for performance, without risking inclusiveness, will eventually crash. In an environment of safety, exhibit the courage to risk sharing your authentic self. Do it one step at a time—don't throw everything on the table, but gradually reveal the areas where you need support and the areas that reflect your strengths. If you are a primary leader in the relationship, you can cultivate a safe environment by allowing others to honestly appraise your strengths and weaknesses. A safe environment means there is acceptance of insight or opinion without lashing out, even when it is painful. I believe this single idea could radically alter the health of many marriages and working relationships if it were understood and applied.

Question: How does one handle aggressive, hurtful exchanges? A safe environment must be established by the tone setter/leader/friend. Asking questions and intently listening to answers allows others to feel valued. This will help you make an honest appraisal of others' strengths and weaknesses without sending a message of rejection. Always remember: opinions (yours and everyone else's) are formed out of a lifetime of experiences. In all situations, you are dealing with not only the person you see but also that person's past. He or she may be responding to or even echoing choices that previous generations have made. The reasons that bring about aggressive, hurtful exchanges are usually hidden deep in his or her family/generational patterns. A wise leader will patiently and skillfully get from the badly presented issue to the real issue.

Question: What is a solid attitude check? Fundamental in maintaining a positive attitude is understanding one's self and remaining humble. Are we willing to expose ourselves to those around us? Will we allow them to emotionally dissect us? In order for this attitude to be maintained, we need to go beyond the question that dominates our internal conversations: "What's in it for me?" Self-centered actions disrupt every relational environment they dominate. The minute we put our own well-being above those we influence, we forfeit the ability to lead morally. Those around us will feel the disconnect and withdraw emotionally for self-preservation.

Check yourself: the humble attitude is the most positive. It says, "How can I help you be successful?" Positive, reinforcing people provide a productive, fulfilling environment to operate within. It is like fertilizer to a plant. Over time it grows stronger and more fruitful.

Question: OK, how can that realistically happen? It can happen when we choose to move from a performance-based model for life—when we choose to explore ourselves, reveal ourselves, and, in humility, include others in our growth track of personal development.

Observation: It takes time and perseverance to discover who you are and then stay consistent with that discovery. The payoff is the opportunity to become the leader you desire to be.

10

STAYING THE COURSE!

Success is not final, failure is not fatal: it is the
courage to continue that counts.

— WINSTON CHURCHILL

There are three primary detractors that threaten the change process: the hidden influence of our primary role model, the uncertainty and risk of uncovering truth, and the powerful voice of a formulaic guru.

The most important detractor of change is the internal conversation constantly going on in our heads. It is shaped both positively and negatively by our role models. As a man, my dad modeled the principles of masculinity that have guided my life. For most women, mothers are the primary role model. Let's admit it: there were deficits.

Whether our parents were passive or active, disappointment resides deeply in many of us from those years of interaction. They definitely set a tone that guides our internal conversation. How our model processed life has either become a standard to achieve or a standard to make excuses. Discovering whether to embrace or to disrupt the subconscious influence of one's primary mentor is vital in order to begin the journey of achieving change.

Question: How does one contextualize internal conversations? In order to gain an objective perspective of my dad, I had to seek it. To facilitate this quest, I had to be willing to set aside my childish image of Dad in order to hear what others thought he valued and how he impacted them. Acquiring feedback from aunts, uncles, and siblings gave me a context to appraise the reason behind my internal dialogue. My dad was a risk taker, a man without a mature mentor. His father had left him at birth, and his brother, who was three years older, became his model. They were required to provide income for their immigrant mom through selling newspapers, chopping wood, and shoveling snow-covered walkways. There was no childhood for my dad; he had to carry adult responsibility from a very young age. The harshness of his childhood left him little time to contemplate emotions. Following his lead, I also grew up lacking emotional intelligence. I felt deeply, but was often unable to make sense of what I was feeling.

I was a supersensitive kid but felt any show of those emotions was weakness. I had to perform, be responsible, and maintain an exterior of success even when my life was conflicted internally. I see now that stifling my feelings led to a deep sense of insecurity. Performance was how I defined myself. It also directed my internal conversation, which was guided by the principle of competence: "Get it done well; make others feel confident in your performance, and they will not know the void deep inside." I am certain my dad fought this battle also, and after he passed, family members confirmed it.

My father's emotional immaturity showed up in his insistence that others accept his perspective on life. His military background, which I admire, deeply influenced his life. He would often say, "It's not for you to question why; it's just for you to do or die." This helped form how I made decisions. Whenever I contemplated a course of action, the concept of "why" was never a part of my internal discussion. I acted on the impulse of personal desire without caring about the emotional consequence.

As I aged, an awareness of the pain I caused in others forced me to examine why I acted without emotional awareness. I was forced to look at myself through the model given to me by a dad I loved. That presented a practical obstacle for me. It seemed disloyal to speak about him objectively; my immature idea of love overshadowed reality. But when I decided to take the first and most intimidating step—an honest appraisal—things started to make sense. My intention was not to disparage my dad but to understand how the patterns he had honestly come by had found their way into my psyche. I could finally see that along with the weaknesses he passed down to me, he also provided some wonderful strengths. In those early days of change, I found myself studying, as objectively as I could, the context of him.

Happily, instead of feeling I was betraying him, I felt freedom! Seeing him honestly as a dad who was broken, just like the rest of us, helped me finally see the truth about myself. It was then that I became free to change—to break from some of those patterns of internal discussion. I began to take notice that those closest to me, my wife and children, were beginning to relax in the new atmosphere I was providing. I was on a roll! I had become aware and then convinced of a critically important concept: deep internal change occurs when we objectively examine our primary model, understand the context of his or her story, and recognize the impact the generational patterns have had on us.

The second factor that detracts change is risk. As I look back, the risk of upsetting the status quo was very real, but I had come to the place where I was willing to go for it; I had no choice, and there was too much at stake not to.

To this day, when I become aware of a personal challenge and pursue change, it disrupts the lives of those close to me. My change forces them to revisit how they perceive me and how they respond to my freedom. The pushback can be unending and often brutal, especially if it involves fundamental change. I sincerely say that the greatest gift you can give to family and coworkers affected by your change is to consistently live your values when challenged. Speak your mind with kindness and patience. Your journey has not been theirs. They need to see this is not a fad or short-lived awakening. They will be convinced through your altered life patterns, not your words.

The final detractor to change is the voice of the guru. This voice expresses systematic ideas that guide you through a formulaic process which keeps you under their control. A formula rarely produces freedom; it more often creates dependence on another's philosophy of life. Be aware that family, friends, and coworkers may try to use gurus who represent their relational desires to try to manage your freedom. Expect that relational change will put an initial strain on all relationships; my change forces others to either change or walk away. It may lead to a period of chaos. In the middle of change, doubt can become others' ally and your nemesis. I suggest that once you set your course, keep your path to change simple and unencumbered by intellectual clutter.

Keep in mind that success is not measured by daily or weekly outcomes, but by what it takes to stop you. In the necessary process of change, you will need to explore and then struggle against what threatens to stop you: internal voices, fear of risk, and external voices.

Observation: The road to change will be challenged by internal and external road blocks. Freedom is at stake. Move forward with resolve!

FINAL THOUGHTS

By now you realize that objective self-evaluation is not for the weak-willed. As you make a commitment to personal development and couple it with patience, risk, perseverance, and resilience, the gap that exists between strength and vulnerability will close. Your personal identity and its influence on others are at stake.

The process begins with your willingness to examine your past, embrace your core values, and understand how you impact those around you. The inclusion of others as you move forward will create a momentum that will challenge and change your relationships at home, at work, and in your social circle.

Your ultimate challenge in bridging the gap between strength and vulnerability will be this: balancing your desire to perform with the maintenance of your core values. Remember that the accurate evaluation of one's self cannot be done in a vacuum; it will best be accomplished with the help of carefully chosen wise people.

Go to work. Personalize the concepts. Reread until the flow begins to impact your closest relationships. As you move forward, remember this is not a formula, but a relational construct built to serve your personal development.

Contributors to the development of the ideas contained in the book are as follows:

Discussions with Arlis Hettinga Urcavich, 1968–2015, Collierville, TN

Discussions with Dr. Basil Jackson, 1987–2005, Milwaukee, WI

Discussions with Brent Causey, 2003–2015, San Antonio, TX

Discussions with Bruce Conger, 1977–2015, Green Bay, WI

Discussions with Chris Olson Utech, 1987–2015, Green Bay, WI

Discussions with Dawn Urcavich McKay, 1973–2015, Germantown, TN

Discussions with Dr. Denver Johnson, 1993–2015, Green Bay, WI

Discussions with Fred Busch, 1968-2015, Safety Harbor, FL

Discussions with Jerry Price, 1967–2015, Phoenix, AZ

Discussions with Joan Mays Johnson, 1993–2015, Green Bay, WI

Discussions with Joe DeLisi, 2009–2015, Collierville, TN

Discussions with Joe Urcavich Jr., 1977–2015, Germantown, TN

Discussions with Ken Utech, 1987–2015, Green Bay, WI

Discussions with Pete App, 1995–2009, Green Bay, WI

Discussions with Randy Urcavich, 1958–2015, Gwinn, MI

Discussions with Sherri Eisenreich Urcavich, 1999–2015, Germantown, TN

Discussions with Dr. Steve Gerndt, 2002–2015, Green Bay, WI

ABOUT THE AUTHOR

Dr. Joe Urcavich began his career as a high-school history teacher, became a college teacher and sports coach, and then served in a senior-pastor position for thirty years in both Green Bay, Wisconsin, and Collierville, Tennessee. For the past twenty-three years, Joe has worked as a consultant in leadership development.

As a former chaplain for the Green Bay Packers, Joe has a depth of experience with high-profile and high-pressure situations. This experience extends to his work over the past ten years with US Army chaplains and officers in Alaska, Texas, Kansas, Germany, and Washington, DC. He has also served as keynote speaker at corporate events, men's retreats, and marriage conferences. Currently he is a public speaker, leadership coach, and alignment advisor.

Joe resides in Collierville, Tennessee, with Arlis, his wife of forty-five years. His greatest pleasure is interacting on a daily basis with their adult children and six grandsons. Golf, reading, and travel are his passions.

Joe's website: josephurcavich.com

Made in the USA
Middletown, DE
21 July 2015